God Is Like a Video Game

30-Day Devotional for Those Looking to Level Up Their Character

Chris Stanley

Stanley Crew Publishing

Contents

INTRODUCTION

You know the story, there's a girl. She's a princess in a faraway land and there is a guy that's crazy about her. They have had a miraculous meeting and fall in love. They plan on getting married and living happily ever after.

Everything is great, except there is a bad guy. He's got horns, evil minions, and he hates the guy who has fallen in love. The bad guy steals the princess and takes her to his evil lair of fire and waits for his enemy to come and try to save her.

This hero loves the princess so much that he fights through hordes of evil minions level after level to save her. When the hero reaches the bad guy, he deals a crushing blow to the boss and takes back his princess.

They live happily ever after, that is until the sequel hits and something goes wrong… again.

That princess is always getting into trouble and our mustachioed hero keeps fighting for her no matter how many times she finds herself in danger.

You probably know this story, it is the story of Mario and his beloved Princess Peach, but it is also the story of Jesus and His princess and soon to be bride, the church.

Husbands, love your wives, just as Christ loved the church and gave himself up for her,

26 in order to make her holy by cleansing her with the washing of water by the word,

27 so as to present the church to himself in splendor, without a spot or wrinkle or anything of the kind— yes, so that she may be holy and without blemish.
- Ephesians 5:25 27 (ESV)

As I review this story, I'm shocked at how similar the story of Mario and Jesus is. In fact, the only difference is one story is make believe, and the other is true. Both Mario and Jesus start out as everyday Joes and turn into extraordinary heroes.

In this book, we'll be exploring different ways that God is like a video game. Through the history of video games, we'll be dwelling on the creator of the universe through this popular pastime. We've broken the book into four parts for you.

In part one of the book, we'll start off with "The Characters." Here we'll dive into the cast of God's story by comparing them to the cast of popular video games. I titled the second part of the book "How to Play." There we'll cover some things you must know about video games and

God before you dive into actually playing. Inside of the third section we'll cover "Game Mechanics." Here we'll explain how things work inside of a game so we can better understand God. We'll wrap up in part four by looking at some specific game examples and what they can teach us about God and His character.

God is our hero, He is our savior, He loves and cares for us, He'll fight for us to the end, no matter how many times we find ourselves in trouble. God is like a video game.

The Characters

Part 1

#01 Hero

During the 1980s, a Japanese toy company, Nintendo, was on the brink of disaster. Their company had charged forward into the technological era of video games. They'd seen some minor success, but they needed a big win in North America as they faced financial ruin.

Nintendo reassured their salespeople that they had a new game that would change their company's fate. When it arrived, the North American sales team anxiously waited while the arcade game powered on. As the screen came to life, they saw a big monkey grab a girl and climb some ladders. The girl's presumed boyfriend, a blue-collar worker, had to navigate construction sites and avoid objects thrown at him by the big ape while trying to save his girlfriend.

It dismayed the sales team. They'd hoped for a racing game or something more attractive than a big overgrown monkey and a guy in overalls. What was Nintendo corporate thinking? How could this new game, titled Donkey Kong, and the mustached hero save their company?

It turned out, Nintendo was right. Donkey Kong and the mustached hero went on to not only save Pauline, the damsel in distress, but saved Nintendo. Eventually, that little unnamed mustached carpenter became one of the biggest video game icons of all time. He soon became known as Mario. Along with his fame came a change of professions. He went from being a carpenter to a plumber.

Nintendo's sales team was apprehensive because they thought they knew what they needed, a game that was exciting and attractive. They had never envisioned that the game to save their job would look like Mario and Donkey Kong. Their expectations were all wrong.

The New Testament talks about how the Jews of the day were waiting and looking for a savior. They believed that the redeemer they were waiting for would free them from Roman rule. Because they were waiting for a politician or a conqueror, the Jews completely missed the coming of Jesus, who was their long-prophesied savior.

Even those closest to Jesus struggled when Jesus didn't fulfill what they thought He should be doing. While John the Baptist (Jesus' cousin) was in prison, John sent word to Jesus, asking if He was the Messiah.

---

2 When John, who was in prison, heard about the deeds of the Messiah, he sent his disciples 3 to ask him, "Are you the one who is to come, or should we expect someone else?"

4 Jesus replied, "Go back and report to John what you hear and see:

5 The blind receive sight, the lame walk, those who have leprosy are cleansed, the deaf hear, the dead are raised, and the good news is proclaimed to the poor.

6 Blessed is anyone who does not stumble on account of me."
- Matthew 11:2-6 (NIV)

As Christians, we often doubt that Jesus is really the Savior because life gets hard, we get scared, and we want our Savior to come down and rescue us from our circumstances.

Those in Jesus' hometown doubted as well,

---

53 When Jesus had finished these parables, he moved on from there.

54 Coming to his hometown, he began teaching the people in their synagogue, and they were amazed. "Where did this man get this wisdom and these miraculous powers?" they asked.

55 "Isn't this the carpenter's son? Isn't his mother's name Mary, and aren't his brothers James, Joseph, Simon and Judas?

56 Aren't all his sisters with us? Where then did this man get all these things?" 57 And they took offense at him.
- Matthew 13:53-57 (NIV)

The reality is God didn't send Jesus to free John from prison or to free the Jews from Rome. God wanted to save our souls, and to do that, God sent a humble carpenter to save us, His girl, His future bride.

Just like Nintendo's sales team didn't see a savior when they saw a carpenter, so too did the Jews overlook the Savior of the world because all they saw was a carpenter named Jesus.

#02 Princess

Princess Peach, also known as Princess Toadstool, is a staple of Nintendo's Mario games. Most know the Princess as sweet, well mannered, and a little naïve. She is always getting into trouble and cannot seem to help herself.

Mario loves Peach, like absolutely loves her and never gives up on her, even though she's a lot of trouble. He seems to always be running around chasing after her, trying to save her from the evil bad guy.

Peach doesn't seem to love Mario as much, yet this doesn't sway Mario from risking life and limb repeatedly to save his love.

The Bible talks about how the church, that is you and I, are betrothed to Christ.

---

2 For I feel a divine jealousy for you, since I betrothed you to one husband, to present you as a pure virgin to Christ.

3 But I am afraid that as the serpent deceived Eve by his cunning, your thoughts will be led astray from a sincere and pure devotion to Christ.
- 2 Corinthians 11:2-4 (ESV)

The church belongs to Christ, and He is coming to take us back to His magical kingdom to marry His bride.

Whether it is Israel in the Old Testament or us in our individual lives, we seem to be just like Princess Peach, always getting into trouble. Whether we are naïve or just don't care as much for Christ as He does for us, Jesus still shows up to save the day.

For the Son of Man came to seek and to save the lost.
- Luke 19:10

We fall prey to the enemy's tricks and schemes, then act surprised. We know there is an enemy out to destroy us, but just like Peach we do little to avoid him.

Now Princess Peach has her own powers. She has the power of light, love or various other versions depending on the game. In one game, Bowser stole Princess Peach because she is the only one that could oppose him and stop his reign of darkness. She scared him.

The Bible talks about how we are the light of the world and how we should shine before men.

14 "You are the light of the world...

16 In the same way, let your light shine before others, that they may see your good deeds and glorify

Part of the reason Satan does so much to stop us is because our ability to shine light into darkness scares him. We are the only way people see Jesus on Earth, and until Christ comes back, we are God's weapon for opposing the darkness.

Just like Mario must save Princess Peach, so too does God deliver us from our sin and the enemy of our souls.

#03 Villain

Whether it is Bowser in Mario, Ganondorf in Zelda, Joker in Batman, or even the ultimate baddie, Sephiroth in Final Fantasy VII, the bad guys cannot leave the good guys alone.

Why is this? Why does Bowser want to steal Peach? Why does Sephiroth (spoiler alert if you have never played it) kill the innocent Aerith?

Because that is what bad guys do… right? It isn't that simple. Most often it is because they hate the hero or good that stands in their way of achieving what they want.

Bowser and Ganondorf want to rule over the kingdoms. Sephiroth believes he is god and wants to rule the world. Whatever good or innocence stands in the way of them achieving their ultimate bad guy goal is what they'll fight.

The Bible talks about how we have an enemy of our souls who is Lucifer or Satan. Now, like Sephiroth, Lucifer wasn't always a bad guy. In fact, the Bible tells that Lucifer was one of God's angels.

Although some bad guys need radiation or some other type of chemical reaction to turn them into villains, Satan was infected with pride. He didn't want to serve God; he wanted to be God.

---

13 You said in your heart, I will ascend to heaven; above the stars of God. I will set my throne on high; I will sit on the mount of assembly in the far reaches of the

north;

14 I will ascend above the heights
of the clouds; I will make myself
like the Most High.'
- Isaiah 14:13-14 (ESV)

It was for this that God threw Lucifer out of heaven and banished him to the Earth. Lucifer didn't give up at that point, oh no.

Satan was insulted that God had placed man above angels as the inheritor of God's kingdom. Can you imagine! Pitiful man to be above angels.

Do you not know that we will judge angels?
- 1st Corinthians 6:3 (NIV)

You can imagine how Lucifer must feel. He's gone from being a high-ranking angel, thinking he should rule all of heaven, to now being below mortal man.

Satan devises a plan to trick God's chosen bride to give up the keys to the kingdom and our relationship with God. Why? Because it is the only way to get back at God and start his climb back to power.

His plan worked. In the Garden of Eden, he tricked us into disobeying and separating ourselves from God creating darkness and sin.

We believed Lucifer over God, putting Satan in power and pulling us into a rebellion against God on Earth. Jesus later won back His bride with the cross, but Satan is still trying to ruin the relationship between man and God whenever he can. Pushing us to sin, to let darkness in our lives so we will reject and hide from God once again.

> *This is the verdict: Light has come into the world, but people loved darkness instead of light because their deeds were evil.*
> *-John 3:19 (NIV)*

> *Your enemy the devil prowls around like a roaring lion looking for someone to devour. Resist him, standing firm in the faith.*
> *- 1 Peter 5:8-9*

Just like bad guys want to steal away the loved one of the hero, become king, or create darkness, so does the enemy of God and our soul try to do everything he can to bring darkness into our world and our souls.

#04 Duo's

Mario, originally named Jumpman, saved Nintendo with his leading role in Donkey Kong. After this, Nintendo realized they had a star on their hands.

They began creation of a game that would further showcase their jumping hero. The lead creator of the game, Shigeru Miyamoto, felt they needed to add a second playable character. Enter Luigi, Mario's brother, and the name of Mario's new game, "Super Mario Bros."

Since 1983 Mario and Luigi have been near inseparable as they've conquered bigger and bigger challenges, world after world, and game after game. Gamers love Luigi. The Mario brothers duo has become the most popular series of all time.

Duos have made video games more enjoyable, sociable, and easier to play. Other popular video game duos are Sonic and Tails, the brothers in Double Dragon, Ken and Ryu of Street Fighter, Donkey and Diddy Kong, Banjo and Kazooie, Ratchet and Clank, and Jak and Daxter.

When a world needs saving, sending more than just one person seems to be the way to go. Jesus also sent out His disciples two by two to reach the world.

And he called his twelve disciples
together and began sending them
out two by two, giving them
authority to cast out evil spirits.
- Mark 6:7 (NLT)

There is power in not being alone. There is accountability to keep each other on mission. There is help and support if something goes wrong, and comradery if things get tough.

9 Two are better than one,
because they have a good return
for their labor:

10 If either of them falls down,
one can help the other up. But pity
anyone who falls and has no one to
help them up.

11 Also, if two lie down together,
they will keep warm. But how can
one keep warm alone?

12 Though one may be
overpowered, two can defend
themselves. A cord of three strands

is not quickly broken.
- Ecclesiastes 4:9-12 (NIV)

The Bible highlights relationships between Paul and Timothy, Paul and Silas, Peter James and John, Moses and Aaron, David and Jonathon.

Just like Nintendo knew Mario was better off with Luigi and Sega knew Sonic needed Tails, so too God knew we'd need each other and be better off two by two.

#05 Relatable Characters

You slice through the evil dragon and watch him disappear from the screen. You reap your reward of gold, EXP, and a rare item. Pocketing your goodies and running across the desert, you spot a character fighting a baddie. You observe their fight and after the death of the enemy; the character runs off.

There is a character sitting next to a stream, probably fishing. Another is sitting at the entrance to town selling items and potions.

One of the coolest things about RPG and open world video games has always been the NPC's, or non-playable characters. They have a limited script and it always leave you wanting to know more about their story, but there is no way to find out more.

With the invention of the internet and massively multiplayer online games, or MMO's, nearly every character represents a person. These characters are no longer scripted sprites on a screen, behind each one is an actual human being. They have families, hopes, fears, dreams, aspirations, concerns, and most of all a story.

Often, in our own lives, we live in a first-person perspective. We see the world through our own eyes, and we are the star of our own game.

We imagine we are like Cloud, Mario, or Sonic and it is our job to survive this life and everyone else is just watching us. We run right past other people we see and don't give it a second thought. They feel like NPC's to us, like they aren't genuine people.

The old white guy sitting by himself in the corner booth. What is his story? The Hispanic teen, he has a full life to worry about just like you. Or the scared mom trying to take care of two children on her own. She has a story. These are your neighbors.

Jesus is talking with a crowd, and someone asks what the most important commandment is. Jesus answers,

---

*29 "The most important one,"
answered Jesus, "is this...*

*30 Love the Lord your God with all
your heart and with all your soul
and with all your mind and with all
your strength.*

*31 The second is this: 'Love your
neighbor as yourself.
- Mark 12:29-31*

Let's define the word neighbor. A neighbor is someone that lives near you. If you are seeing a person in your life, they are your neighbor and God wants you to love them.

They aren't bits of code. They are real live human beings that God created, and He loves them just like you.

---

*34 A new command I give you:
Love one another. As I have loved
you, so you must love one another.
- John 13:34 (NIV)*

Just like video games now have characters online that represent live human beings, so too did God place other people on our planet that represent human souls He called us to love.

How to Play

Part 2

#06 Go All In

People love to play videos games, a lot. We get it, but in 2012 someone went all in.

Okan Kaya broke the longest video game marathon by playing Call of Duty: Black Ops 2, for over 135 hours and in doing so broke the Guinness Book of World Records.

This may seem extreme, but most gamers are extreme. They give their time, heart, mind, effort, money, and sleep all to this addictive pastime.

On average, 18-24-year-olds spend nearly 5 ½ hours a week playing videos games. During the coronavirus lockdown, that number skyrocketed to over 8 hours a week of game time.

One analyst observed that since the highly popular game World of Warcraft released in 2004, humanity has spent nearly 6 million years of collective time playing the game.

In 2013, 30% of the players reported playing over 30hrs a week of WoW. (World of Warcraft) What drives these intense playing sessions and dedication?

Because video games are progressive, we feel we are accomplishing something. We feel successful, like we've achieved something. Dopamine, a feel good chemical, causes these feelings by releasing into the brain when we beat the biggest bad guy or get a new high score.

We search for meaning in life and when the feel-good feeling hits, things make sense, momentarily. We know what to do next, how to accomplish it, and can do good by taking out another baddie.

This feeling of accomplishment and contribution is at least part of the reason we all love video games. Life is hard and we often feel like there is no point to it. Stress builds up to pass school, pay bills, or raise kids, but video games make sense.

All of this combined causes extreme devotion to a hobby which is now turning into a lifestyle for many players.

Often it feels like video game players don't care about work, food, or even where they will sleep. If gaming is happening, they are all good.

This brings to mind what Jesus said,

---

25 "Therefore I tell you, do not worry about your life, what you will eat or drink; or about your body, what you will wear. Is not life more than food, and the body more than clothes?

26 Look at the birds of the air; they do not sow or reap or store away in barns, and yet your heavenly Father feeds them. Are you not much more valuable than they?

27 Can any one of you by worrying add a single hour to your life?
- Matthew 6:25-27 (NIV)

Christ himself called us to a radical devotion where we wouldn't stress about what we eat, drink, or even wear. He wants us to give ourselves up to Him, to trust Him, to give Him everything.

Just like video games cause people to go all in, God is calling us to go all in with Christ.

#07 Marathon

Okan Kayan, that guy who played video games for 135 hours straight, isn't an isolated incident. Gaming marathons are a big deal. There are big events, some even raise money for charity. One charity has raised $28 million dollars in its nine years as an event.

Not all marathons end in smiles, though. One man died during a gaming marathon when he was hoping to set the Guinness Record for playing video games. He isn't the only one. There are others recorded who have died during video game binges or marathons.

The dangers of not moving for tens, if not hundreds of hours, is a real health concern. The blood has trouble flowing and some cause of death has been cold temperatures and over-exhaustion from the long hours spent playing games, likely contributing to cardiac arrest.

Guinness changed the rules to allow players to move 10 minutes in every hour to allow them to get up, stretch, get the blood flowing or even take a nap. A player could decide to accumulate the 10-minute breaks so they could take an extended nap. This is what Okah Kaya used to set the 135-hour record. Okan could keep the blood flowing by getting up and exercising and taking naps with his accumulation of breaks.

Our own Christian walk is similar. We are in our own competition, a race.

> *24 Do you not know that in a race
> all the runners run, but only one
> receives the prize? So run that you
> may obtain it.*
> *- 1st Corinthians 9:24 (ESV)*

This race though is not a sprint, it is a marathon that requires endurance.

> *Therefore, since we are surrounded
> by such a huge crowd of witnesses
> to the life of faith, let us strip off
> every weight that slows us down,
> especially the sin that so easily trips
> us up. And let us run with*
> ***endurance*** *the race God has set
> before us.*
> *- Hebrews 12:1 (NLT)*

There will be times we take it easy, that we take a break, maybe even take a nap. If we sit still for too long, though, we will grow cold.

*12 Because of the increase of wickedness, the **love of most will grow cold**, 13 but the one who stands firm to the end will be saved.*
- Matthew 24:12-13 (NIV)

Just like video gamers competing in a marathon need to endure to the end by staying focused, staying warm, keeping the blood flowing, and sometimes resting, we too must be careful to endure to the end by not letting our love grow cold.

#08 Strategy Guide

As video games became increasingly more difficult to complete, creators started making game strategy guides.

These guides tell the story of the game and the background of the characters. It also gives complete walkthrough tips on how to complete the game, giving clues, hints, and sometimes outright cheats to make the game easier.

Strategy guides show you the enemies and how to defeat them while describing all the different items you can find in the game.

A video game strategy guide is the ultimate way to ensure you survive and complete a game. It makes games that seem impossible become manageable and easy to navigate.

With a strategy guide, you aren't wandering around in circles hoping you are going the right way or working towards the right goals.

In our walk, as Christ following believers, God has given us a strategy guide for living life on Earth. It is called the Bible.

It has extensive back history on all the characters, tells you how to navigate your way through the challenges you'll face, and helps you understand the ultimate goal of the mission you've been given and how to accomplish it.

This Book of the Law shall not depart from your mouth, but you shall meditate on it day and night,

so that you may be careful to do
according to all that is written in it.
For then you will make your way
prosperous, and then you will have
good success.
- Joshua 1:8 (ESV)

God's Law, His word, the Bible, is something that we should review every day. Every time we tackle a new day, it is as if it is a new level. We need God's understanding of what we are going to face, how to face it, and how to lean on Him when times are tough.

When the Spirit of truth comes, he
will guide you into all the truth, for
he will not speak on his own
authority, but whatever he hears he
will speak, and he will declare to
you the things that are to come.
- John 16:13 (ESV)

Just like strategy guides tell a player what to expect and how to beat the game, we also know that God knows the timing, the sequence, and how we can successfully navigate this life into the next.

#09 The Storyline

He pulls the sword out of the innocent one and the victim falls limp.

"No!" screams Cloud as he tries to rush forward to stop it, but he knows he is too late. Sephiroth has won. He has killed innocence as he attempts to become God. He wants to rule the world, and anything that stands in his way will fall by his hand, and the hero hates him for it.

The most crushing part of all of this, Cloud knows he is to blame. He is part of the evil, part of the problem, he is connected to this evil being.

Cloud fights hard every day to shake off the thoughts that are in his head. It is as if Sephiroth is inside of him, calling him to do evil. Cloud knows he is a child of Sephiroth, forever a piece of him, and this makes Cloud fight even harder.

He will avenge the innocent blood that has been spilled, because he must fight the evil he sees to fight the evil inside of himself.

That is one storyline in Final Fantasy VII.

Jesus was killed because of us. He was killed to save us. It was because of our sin that Jesus died on the cross.

We thought he brought it on himself, that God was punishing him for his own failures. But it was our sins that did that to him, that ripped and tore and crushed him— our sins! He took the punishment, and that made us whole. Through his bruises we get healed.
- Isaiah 5:4-5 (MSG)

You might think that it isn't your fault. That you aren't to blame for Jesus' death, but we all are.

23 for all have sinned and fall short of the glory of God,
- Romans 3:23 (NIV)

Before Jesus was killed for our sins, He was distraught at how so many Jews did not believe in His message. He was pleading with them to believe and when they wouldn't believe, He laid this bomb on them.

44 You belong to your father, the devil, and you want to carry out your father's desires. He was a murderer from the beginning
John 8:44 (NIV)

Just like Sephiroth killed innocent people and Cloud had to admit he was part of the problem, we too have to admit we are to blame for Christ being killed on the cross and accept His forgiveness.

#10 Amazing Visuals

About every 7 years, the major video game console creators Sony, Microsoft, and Nintendo release a new console.

Traditionally, the improvements that come from new video game consoles are superior graphics. It needs to feel real, as real as possible. Gamers want to feel involved in the video game not only with the controller they use, but with visuals. With the PS5, the possibility of gaming in 4k exists, which means it'll be extremely immersive.

Console creators showcase beautiful graphics to entice people to buy their console. With $500 as the starting price for the PS5, there must be a compelling reason for someone to want to buy in.

People celebrate Sony, Nintendo, and Microsoft for creating such beautiful environments for them to play in, but how often do we sit back in awe at the amazing world God created for us?

---

3 Through him all things were made; without him nothing was made that has been made.
- John 1:3 (NIV)

When you look around at our planet, it is breathtaking. Stop and look. The sky and the intricate clouds, the birds flying to and froe, the beautiful meadow dotted with brilliant colorful flowers, and don't forget about the night sky.

The reality is console creators are trying to catch up and create beautiful visuals like God does. Every seven years they take a huge leap forward in recreating what God did in seven days.

Just like video game consoles provide beautiful and immersive environments for gamers to interact with, so too did God provide us with the ultimate visuals that provide us with a breathtaking environment to live our lives.

#11 The World

In 2009 video gamers saw a new sandbox-style game released. This game was unlike most games people had ever seen. It seemed clunky, weird, and blocky.

This blockiness didn't stop the world from falling in love with the endless exploration and creation that the game provided. This sandbox game became the best-selling video game of all time by selling 200 million copies. That little game is Minecraft.

The concept of a sandbox game is that the creator has designed a space for the players to create. Think back to a kid in a sandbox where they can do anything they can imagine with the sand and anything they find inside the sandbox: few rules and lots of creative possibilities. Sandbox games spark creativity and pull players in by letting them control what happens.

It allows players to run around and mine various materials and create things with them. They can fight monsters called mobs, build houses, and explore the infinite map they roam.

Players can also choose to enter an empty world where their only job is to create and build. The world is their oyster.

This idea of a massive world, unlimited possibilities, and the players given the keys to the kingdom takes me back to the beginning of our origins when God made Earth.

1 In the beginning God created the heavens and the Earth.

2 Now the Earth was formless and empty, darkness was over the surface of the deep, and the Spirit of God was hovering over the waters.

3 And God said, "Let there be light," and there was light.

4 God saw that the light was good, and he separated the light from the darkness.

5 God called the light "day," and the darkness he called "night." And there was evening, and there was morning—the first day.
- Genesis 1:1-5 (NIV)

God brilliantly created the world. Light careened across space, flowing from the creator of the universe and filled up the Earth.

A few days later, He created us, mankind.

26 Then God said, "Let us make mankind in our image, in our likeness, so that they may rule over the fish in the sea and the birds in the sky, over the livestock and all the wild animals, and over all the creatures that move along the ground."

27 So God created mankind in his own image, in the image of God he created them; male and female he created them.
- Genesis 1:26-27 (NIV)

After God had placed mankind on the planet, He told them to take care of everything He had made.

15 The Lord God took the man and put him in the Garden of Eden to work it and take care of it.
- Genesis 2:15 (NIV)

Earth has been man's ultimate sandbox ever since. We've discovered new ways of doing things. We have improved things, such as transportation, by learning how to make the wheel, chariots, cars, airplanes, and now spaceships.

These things are all made from the essential elements God created and provided us within the Earth.

Just like Minecraft made a place for players to build in with the elements and materials provided, so too did God make a fantastic sandbox for His beloved creation to build in.

#12 Choose Your Path

Being able to choose what to do and when to do it is what some players are into. From open world games like Elder Scrolls and Grand Theft Auto, these types of games allow for nonlinear story lines. They allow players to explore entire cities, countries, and even worlds.

This differs from the olden days of simple arcade games and platform jumping sprites. Players can choose to pursue a certain storyline or just roam about wreaking havoc or hunting treasure. The choice is the player's.

These games attempt to push the player to progress in the story. It will provide hints of the next steps or show the player a reminder of what they need to do. The player may choose to ignore it, but often the game will only let you go so far in exploring. While you can choose to not follow the storyline and do what you want, the game limits your options.

Whether it's super strong bad guys, locked doors, or hidden areas, progressing through the storyline of the game is the only way to explore everything and to open up more options. The creators of the game are always there, subtly prompting you on the next steps to take so you can make progress.

God does the same in our lives. He gives us ultimate freedom to decide. He allows us to make mistakes, to sin, and even cause pain to others. He never forces us to love Him, and He never forces us to go a certain direction. He allows us to choose our own path.

God is always there, letting us know what steps to take
next. We may choose to take one job over another, but
God is there closing and opening doors guiding us towards
His storyline.

When I think of choosing a path, I remember Jonah. Jonah
was God's prophet, God's mouthpiece, and God allowed
Him to run away from His responsibility, but God made it
extremely clear what steps He wanted Jonah to take next.

Jonah had run away on a ship in the opposite direction
God had directed Him to go. When Jonah disobeyed, God
sent a dangerous storm. The sailors cast lots (drew
names) to see who had angered God, and they drew
Jonah's name.

*8 So they asked him, "Tell us, who
is responsible for making all this
trouble for us?...*

*9 He answered, "I am a Hebrew
and I worship the Lord, the God of
heaven, who made the sea and the
dry land."*

*10 This terrified them and they
asked, "What have you done?"
(They knew he was running away*

42

*from the Lord, because he had
already told them so.)*

*11 The sea was getting rougher and
rougher. So they asked him, "What
should we do to you to make the
sea calm down for us?"*

*12 "Pick me up and throw me into
the sea," he replied, "and it will
become calm. I know that it is my
fault that this great storm has come
upon you"*

*...15 Then they took Jonah and
threw him overboard, and the
raging sea grew calm.
Jonah 1:8-15 (NIV)*

You may know the story. A whale swallows Jonah and he
has a choice to make. Go do what God asked Him to do or
sit in a whale. Accept His mission or stay where He was at.

Just like open world video games direct the steps of the
player while still allowing for choices and exploration, so
too does God give us an option of what path to choose
while guiding us on what steps to take next.

Game Mechanics

Part 3

#13 Username

Known by many names such as gamer tags, gamer id's, login credentials, and gamer handle, a username represents your in-game persona. Players base this name on how they see themselves, rather than how they actually are.

Some games, like Minecraft, will auto-generate a name for you when you get started, or you can customize your characters on screen ID to your liking. You can accept "Steve" as your name, or you can go with NinjaBoy2099. You get to give your character whatever name you want.

The Bible talks about how God will give us a new name when we level up into His kingdom.

To the one who is victorious, I will give some of the hidden manna. I will also give that person a white stone with a new name written on it, known only to the one who receives it.
- Revelation 2:17 (NIV)

You and God will have a codename. He's going to customize you and give you a name that represents how much He loves you and what He thinks about you. This is a name that only you and God will know.

Why would God change our name? If we want to understand why God changes names, we can look at an example of Him changing someone's name in the Bible.

Jacob wrestled with an angel of God through the night.

Then the man said, "Let me go, for it is daybreak."

But Jacob replied, "I will not let you go unless you bless me."

27 The man asked him, "What is your name?"

"Jacob," he answered.

28 Then the man said, "Your name will no longer be Jacob, but Israel, because you have struggled with God and with humans and have overcome."
- Genesis 32:26-28

Jacob wrestled with relationships, struggled in life, and even fought with God. This caused God to change his name to something that God thought better represented Jacob's persona.

Just like gamers can change their character's on-screen name to fit their gaming persona, so too will God change our name to match how He sees us through His eyes.

#14 Weapons

The world is spinning. Flashes of light and darkness. The hero lands on his back and has the wind knocked out of him. The light of the sun blinds him.

He squints and remembers what happened. Jumping up, he unsheathes his trusty sword, ready to fend off any attack. He scans the horizon and sees nothing but cows grazing in the pasture.

Our hero has just experienced time travel and is in an unfamiliar place. Or maybe he's lost his memory and experiencing amnesia. One thing is for sure, he's glad he has his weapon.

Whether it's Link's Master Sword in Zelda, Cloud's Buster Sword of Final Fantasy VII, or Mega Man's arm cannon called the Mega Buster, weapons are a big part of video games. They are critical to the hero's survival and vital to vanquishing evil while protecting the one who wields it.

Often to get these weapons, the hero has had to go through a quest to earn it.

Luckily for us, God has also provided us lost and weary souls with weapons for our protection and for battle with the enemy of our soul.

17 Take the helmet of salvation and the sword of the Spirit, which is the word of God.
- Ephesians 6:17

The sword Is Iconic not just in video games but also in Jesus' day. Roman soldiers were a common sight and every time you saw a soldier you saw their sword, but how is the word of God like a sword?

---

12 For the word of God is alive and active. Sharper than any double-edged sword, it penetrates even to dividing soul and spirit, joints and marrow; it judges the thoughts and attitudes of the heart.
- Hebrews 4:12

The word of God, like a sword, can help protect us and vanquish evil from our souls. Remember Jesus in the desert? He was under attack. Satan was tempting Jesus,

---

5 Then the devil took him to the holy city and had him stand on the highest point of the temple. 6 "If you are the Son of God," he said, "throw yourself down. For it is written:

"He will command his angels concerning you,

and they will lift you up in their

hands,

so that you will not strike your foot against a stone."

7 Jesus answered him, "It is also written: 'Do not put the Lord your God to the test.
Matthew 4:5-7 (NIV)

Satan was throwing attack after attack at Jesus, and Jesus was blocking each attack with verses from God's word. Jesus emerged victorious with one powerful swing of the word of God.

---

8 Again, the devil took him to a very high mountain and showed him all the kingdoms of the world and their splendor. 9 "All this I will give you," he said, "if you will bow down and worship me."

10 Jesus said to him, "Away from me, Satan! For it is written: 'Worship the Lord your God, and serve him only."

11 Then the devil left him...
- Matthew 4:8-11 (NIV)

Just like video games give a weapon to the hero for attacking and defending the on screen enemies so too does God give us weapons to defend our souls and to eliminate evil from our lives.

#15 Armor

You're sweating bullets as the evil Piglin is smacking you with his sword while another pegs you with arrows from a distance. It isn't for this reason that you're sweating, it's the lava you're sitting in. "Player tried to swim in lava" pops up on screen thanks to your float into the fiery liquid in Minecraft's Nether dimension.

Death doesn't scare you, you know your character will just respawn, but you could lose your beautiful armor. Good thing you upgraded your diamond armor into Netherite armor just before you tackled this quest.

Protecting yourself in video games is important. Most games offer shields, helmets, breastplates, or some combination of armor. Armor is there to protect a warrior in battle.

There are many types of armor in history. The Chinese used layers of rhinoceros skins as armor in the 11th century and the Mongols used ox skin in the 13th century. The middle ages saw chain mail become the standard armor. Eventually, full plated armor became the go to protection in the 14th and 15th centuries.

Most armor consists of pieces to protect the chest, head, arms, and legs. Also, warriors need a belt to hang their sword on when not in battle.

Let's get real for a second though, armor just isn't about protecting yourself in games. There is a coolness factor. You want to look the part when you walk out and face the ultimate baddie. You aren't a noob with a leather belt on, (or rhino skin if you are Chinese) you've got the good stuff. As history progressed, armor became a status symbol, and it is no different in video games.

Good armor is treasured and sought after. Plus, it makes you look, well, awesome. Whether it's the Daedric Armor of Elder Scrolls, StarCraft's Powered Combat Suit, or even Super Mario Bros Hammer Suit, looking good while being protected makes getting the best armor worth the work it takes.

Armor can turn the tide of a game for you. What used to be impossible to get across feels like a breeze. What used to kill you in one or two hits, you can now withstand. Armor not only protects you and makes you look cool, it helps you accomplish the mission.

The Bible talks about the importance of putting on the full armor of God.

10 Finally, be strong in the Lord and in his mighty power.

11 Put on the full armor of God, so that you can take your stand against the devil's schemes.

12 For our struggle is not against flesh and blood, but against the rulers, against the authorities, against the powers of this dark world and against the spiritual forces of evil in the heavenly realms.

13 Therefore put on the full armor of God, so that when the day of evil comes, you may be able to stand your ground, and after you have

done everything, to stand.
- Ephesians 6:10-13 (NIV)

God inspired Paul to write those words to a group of believers long ago, and they continue to instruct us today. God, through Paul, is telling us He knows this is a big battle we face, but stand strong. He knows there are hordes of enemies in front and all around us, but suit up and stand strong, rely on Him, and when all else fails trust Him by standing.

I love how God reminds us that the battle isn't against people. That friend of yours you are having so much trouble with? Maybe a family member is just totally being a pain? Don't have enough money? Stressed out in school? Whatever is going on remember that the battle you are facing is not against flesh and blood. It is spiritual. When you feel you are in battle (which is daily!) remember to suit up and rely on God.

Paul goes into detail about the armor of God and each piece's function in our spiritual battles.

14 Stand firm then, with the belt of truth buckled around your waist, with the breastplate of righteousness in place,

15 and with your feet fitted with the readiness that comes from the gospel of peace.

16 In addition to all this, take up

the shield of faith, with which you
can extinguish all the flaming
arrows of the evil one.

17 Take the helmet of salvation and
the sword of the Spirit, which is the
word of God.

18 And pray in the Spirit on all
occasions with all kinds of prayers
and requests.
Ephesians 6:14-18

First is the belt of truth. If you don't have a belt, you can't hold a sword! Truth is in God's word and if you don't know the truth, you cannot be fighting with God's sword of the spirit.

The breastplate of righteousness is your primary defense. It protects your heart, but how can you protect your heart if you aren't living "right" or righteously. Living in sin is a sure way to make your heart vulnerable.

Your shoes, the gospel of peace, protect your feet and are there to make sure you are carrying the message. That you are walking the right mission, and that you know what that mission is. If you don't know your mission, (to bring peace through the gospel) how can you accomplish it?

Your shield of faith is there for when the enemy brings fiery arrows of doubt in your life. When you doubt you can rely on your faith in God to protect you.

Your helmet of salvation is there to protect your mind. With salvation comes a renewing of the mind. While you are surrendering your mind to God, He'll protect your thoughts from the enemy.

I love how Paul ends with, "and pray in the spirit on all occasions." Why is this? We often miss this, we quote the armor verse and walk away, but this is key!

Armor without going to battle is a waste of time. Prayer is how we go to war. It isn't by debating right and wrong. It isn't by preaching fire and brimstone, it's by praying to God. Want to win the battle? You've got to pray.

Just like video games provide the player armor to protect them from the bad guys, so too does God provide us with a sweet suit of armor that will protect us from the attacks of the enemy, if we'll seek after it and put it on.

#16 1-Up

The hero's quest often takes him or her through dangers unimaginable. Evil lords and enemies wait around every corner, pipe, and trash can.

Death is near certain for the hero of the story, but luckily for video gamers there is the valuable 1-Up.

Sometimes represented as hearts or mushrooms, the 1-Up gives the hero an opportunity to try again if they make a fatal error. Whether being smashed by big bricks or falling off the ledge and plunging into darkness, the 1-Up gives them a new opportunity.

These 1-Ups are usually scarce and hidden from view. The player must explore around the entire game searching for where to find this do-over opportunity. In Super Mario Brothers, there are invisible blocks that hide these items. Until the player hits the block, the 1-Up is hidden from view. Once the player discovers it, they receive the extra life. The game often presents these just before or during the hardest parts of the game.

God has given us a 1-Up in His son Jesus Christ. No matter how severe our mess ups, no matter how far we've fallen, Jesus is ready to give you a restart.

If we confess our sins, He is faithful and just to forgive us our sins and to cleanse us from all unrighteousness.
-1st John 1:9 (ESV)

During our life, we may not see Jesus with our physical eyes, He is there like the invisible blocks waiting for us along our path.

Many times, we discover Christ's forgiveness right after we've hit a tremendous obstacle in life. Like a boss battle that has left us weak, we are hanging on by a thread. During the struggle we discover God's redeeming heart not a second too soon.

The Lord is not slow to fulfill his promise as some count slowness, but is patient toward you, not wishing that any should perish, but that all should reach repentance.
- 2nd Peter 3:9

God gives us this extra life so we can avoid death, have life, and finish the level.

Just like 1-Ups are used to give players a 2nd chance, so too does God give us an extra life, an opportunity at a do-over through His son Jesus Christ.

#17 Superstar

There is a battle ahead, a long line of bandits standing between the hero and his goal. Traps below, bullets above, enemies all around, and death near.

The hero needs a miracle, there is no way they can reach the end… maybe this is the end.

He sprints towards the first bad guy and bounces off him into a bonus block that spits out a shiny object. It heads towards the edge of the cliff.

Scrambling and sliding into this pulsing star, the hero gets a surge of adrenaline. He turns to see the obstacles in front of him and realizes, he is invincible.

Charging towards the line of enemies with reckless abandon, he smashes them with relative ease. With one brush of his hand, they fall in defeat.

Along with being invincible, the character speeds up and has an ultimate focus on the prize. If he wastes this opportunity, his quest may end, he must make it to the goal, he must not squander these moments.

This ultimate bonus item, the Superstar, doesn't last forever, but when it comes it delivers the hero from his circumstances. It takes a difficult situation and makes you wonder why the hero was ever worried.

You who sit down in the High God's presence, spend the night in Shaddai's shadow,

Say this: "God, you're my refuge. I trust in you and I'm safe!"

That's right—he rescues you from hidden traps, shields you from deadly hazards. His huge outstretched arms protect you— under them you're perfectly safe; his arms fend off all harm.

Fear nothing—not wild wolves in the night, not flying arrows in the day, Not disease that prowls through the darkness, not disaster that erupts at high noon.

Even though others succumb all around, drop like flies right and left, no harm will even graze you. You'll stand untouched, watch it all from a distance, watch the wicked turn into corpses.

Yes, because God's your refuge, -Psalm 91:1-9 (NIV)

Imagine this scene. Jesus having just showed up to start His ministry, is preaching to the crowds in His hometown of Nazareth.

> *28 All the people in the synagogue were furious when they heard this.*
>
> *29 They got up, drove him out of the town, and took him to the brow of the hill on which the town was built, in order to throw him off the cliff.*
>
> *30 But he walked right through the crowd and went on his way.*
> *- Luke 4:28-30 (NIV)*

He walked right through the crowd and went on His way. Dang. Was Jesus granted a Superstar? I doubt that some shiny pulsing star came bouncing in to save the day, but Jesus was given the ability to walk right through certain death and come out unharmed.

It wasn't His time, God had His back. I think Paul states it perfectly in Romans when he says,

> *31 What then shall we say to these things? If God is for us, who can be*

against us?
- Romans 8:31 (NIV)

We all will die at some point, but God has called us to something. He's called us to do something, to be a part of something, and until He calls us home and says our time is up God has granted us Superstars. We are invincible to death. It has no power over us.

...Death has been swallowed up in victory."

55 "Where, O death, is your victory? Where, O death, is your sting?"

56 The sting of death is sin, and the power of sin is the law.

57 But thanks be to God! He gives us the victory through our Lord Jesus Christ.
- 1st Corinthians 15:54-56 (NIV)

Just like Superstars make the hero invincible to the dangers around them, so too does God make us invincible to the dangers of death. We should charge forward with reckless abandon, keeping our eye on the prize.

#18 HP

Flying onto the screen is the hero's nemesis. Our hero grits his teeth and clutches his sword tighter. He is under attack. Jumping to one side, he narrowly avoids being struck.

A second melee attack lands on the hero and the screen flashes red. The controlling player glances at the bottom of the screen to see he only has 2HP left. One more hit and it is game over.

HP stands for Health or Hit Points. It is an indicator of how much more your character can withstand. In video games mushrooms and others types of foods, potions, magic spells, and even sleep replenish health points.

If a player is unaware of the health of their character, they are certain to find a "Game Over" screen flash up more than once. When getting low on health, players often get more strategic, trying to avoid conflict until they can heal up.

Running away and finding a bed can be a smart move if your health is running low. Just charging in and attacking a group of baddies when your health is low isn't always the best tactic for survival.

Jesus told us In Matthew,

---

*Are you tired? Worn out? Burned out on religion? Come to me. Get away with me and **you'll recover your life.***
- Matthew 11:28 (MSG)

When we visit with God and rest with Him, He will give us everything we need to accomplish what He is asking of us.

I can do all things through him who strengthens me.
- Philippians 4:3 (NIV)

Just like a video game character needs rest to restore his health, so too do we need to take rest and recharge our health by getting away and spending time with God.

#19 MP

The world is ending. The bad guys are closing in and there seems to be no hope for escape.

The enemies outnumber the heroes. No amount of sword swinging or jumping on top of the bad guy's head will make them go away. The hero needs a miracle.

Just then the hero unleashes a ferocious attack. This isn't just any normal attack, it is a special attack. Reserved for select circumstances, this move is only available by saving up and using MP, magic points.

Magic points gradually increase and players earn them through leveling up. Most characters don't have unlimited magic points, and smart players reserve it for those special moments when they need it most.

After using a lot of MP, a character will need to recharge their MP before they can do any more special moves. MP is often only filled back up over time, through potions, or in some games my meditating or "charging up."

After Jesus performed miracles, he would often slip away to pray and be restored by God.

Jesus was performing miracles when He found out that John the Baptist, His cousin and friend, had been killed.

---

13 When Jesus heard what had happened, he withdrew by boat privately to a solitary place.
- Matthew 14:13 (NIV)

Right after this rest, Jesus fed 5000 people with five loaves and two fish. This miracle came after Jesus had time to be with God.

---

15 Yet the news about him spread all the more, so that crowds of people came to hear him and to be healed of their sicknesses.

16 But Jesus often withdrew to lonely places and prayed.
- Luke 5:15-16

It is through the getting away and praying that Jesus could restore His spiritual strength so He could accomplish what He needed to.

Just like video game characters don't have unlimited MP to do unlimited magic or special moves, so too did Jesus need to recharge His MP, His miracle points.

#20 EXP

As video games become bigger and more complex, video game makers face a challenge. How do they make sure the player doesn't die in a matter in of minutes?

One way creators manage this challenge is by making the game change with the user. As the user gets more experience the difficulty of the game increases. The gamers experience is measured through the on-screen character's EXP points.

As the hero defeats monsters, they earn EXP as a reward for winning the encounter. These experience points add up to help the character level up. The leveling up increases various attributes of the players like strength, speed, power, etc.

Some games have "random encounters." Invisible bad guys that randomly pop up to fight the hero. While at first the new player may wander around unsure what a bad guy even looks like, the player learns how the game operates and what to expect. Often, they learn how to avoid encounters with bad guys they don't want to fight again

As we mature in our Christian walk, we are also leveling up in a spiritual sense. New Christians often walk around blindly, unsure about what is good or evil.

The author of Hebrews addresses this in chapter 5.

---

12 In fact, though by this time you ought to be teachers, you need someone to teach you the elementary truths of God's word all over again. You need milk, not solid

food!

*13 Anyone who lives on milk, being
still an infant, is not acquainted
with the teaching about
righteousness.*

*14 But solid food is for the mature,
who by constant use have trained
themselves to distinguish good from
evil.*
- Hebrews 5:12-14 (NIV)

The longer we are Christians, the more we experience God's love, the more we encounter the evil in the world, it all adds up to leveling up in our relationship with God.

We view everything through a more mature lens. We understand what is good and evil. We learn how to avoid encounters with sin and how to defeat the random encounters we have with our flesh.

Just like videos games reward a player with EXP as they encounter bad guys, so too God rewards us with higher levels of maturity as we encounter and defeat the sin in our own lives.

#21 Loot

You finish off the last of the bad guys. You put away your sword, walk to the chest in the corner of the room, and open it up. Inside are bones and rotting flesh, golden horse armor, and a saddle.

This is looting. You can also break blocks and find resources that help you craft new items or build stuff. Looting is one of the most rewarding types of actions inside of games.

These looting and harvesting systems keep a player exploring long after beating the primary storyline to get rare items or armor.

With God, it is similar. The more often you explore our world, the more you read and learn about God, the more nuggets and things you will find about God.

> 44 "The kingdom of Heaven is like treasure hidden in a field. When a man found it, he hid it again, and then in his joy went and sold all he had and bought that field.
> - Matthew 13:44 (NIV)

Jesus told the story of the treasure as a parable. He explained to the disciples that He shares parables so only the chosen will understand the true meaning. The Bible says that God chooses to conceal things for a reason.

*It is the glory of God to conceal
things, but the glory of kings is to
search things out.
- Proverbs 25:2 (ESV)*

There are gems we discover while reading the Bible.
These treasures are life lessons that change who we are,
and we can pass them on to others, including our children.

*The secret things belong to the Lord
our God, but the things that are
revealed belong to us and to our
children forever, that we may do all
the words of this law.
- Deuteronomy 29:29 (NIV)*

Jesus encourages us to seek out Biblical plunder in His
Word.

*7 "Ask and it will be given to you;
seek and you will find; knock and
the door will be opened to you. 8*

*For everyone who asks receives;
the one who seeks finds; and to the
one who knocks, the door will be
opened.
- Matthew 7:7-8 (NIV)*

Just like games encourage players to keep exploring, seeking, and finding things through a loot system, so too does God call you to seek after Him so you can uncover the loot He has for you.

The Games

Part 4

#22 Role Playing Games

1997 changed the video game world for many players. A little RPG (role playing game) named Final Fantasy VII exposed millions of people to this increasingly popular style of game.

What had been a niche group of video gamers that enjoyed RPG's, Final Fantasy VII brought it mainstream to the world. It has remained one of the most popular RPG's over the years.

From sword wielding warriors, healing mages, knuckle busting brawlers, long distance archers to gun blasting soldiers and thiefs, the combination of various types of party members is a key component to the strategy while playing an RPG. Understanding each of the characters and their role and learning how to achieve balance across your on-screen team becomes important as you progress through the game.

There are similar roles and classes of people inside of the church that make up the body of Christ. Paul talks about the various types in 1st Corinthians,

---

8 To one there is given through the Spirit a message of wisdom, to another a message of knowledge by means of the same Spirit,

9 to another faith by the same Spirit, to another gifts of healing by that one Spirit, 10 to another miraculous powers, to another prophecy, to another distinguishing

*between spirits, to another
speaking in different kinds of
tongues, and to still another the
interpretation of tongues.*

*11 All these are the work of one
and the same Spirit, and he
distributes them to each one, just
as he determines.
- 1st Corinthians 12:8-11 (NIV)*

While those in the church may not carry around a gigantic sword in service or have mystical lettering flying around them while they pray, these various gifts of the spirit and roles inside the church are present and needed.

---

*12 Just as a body, though one, has
many parts, but all its many parts
form one body, so it is with Christ.*

*13 For we were all baptized by one
Spirit so as to form one body—
whether Jews or Gentiles, slave or
free—and we were all given the one
Spirit to drink.*

*14 Even so the body is not made up
of one part but of many.
- 1st Corinthians 12:12-14 (NIV)*

Paul was seeing division in the church over the different gifts and functions in the body and was calling the church to unity.

He wraps up the chapter with firm clarity that each person has a different role, but the church needs all of them.

---

27 Now you are the body of Christ, and each one of you is a part of it.

28 And God has placed in the church first of all apostles, second prophets, third teachers, then miracles, then gifts of healing, of helping, of guidance, and of different kinds of tongues.

29 Are all apostles? Are all prophets? Are all teachers? Do all work miracles? 30 Do all have gifts of healing? Do all speak in tongues? Do all interpret? 31 Now eagerly desire the greater gifts.
- 1st Corinthians 12:27-31 (NIV)

Just like in RPG's, there are different roles for those that work miracles, those that heal, or those that do battle, God also has given different roles and abilities to those inside of His church.

#23 3 Dimensions

Found inside of the Minecraft video game are three dimensions.

First, there is the Overworld. This is where the character starts and where the player spends most of their time playing. In the Overworld, the player explores, discovers, creates, and most importantly, survives.

The second dimension is the Nether. The Nether is a dimension filled with fire, lava, and weird fungi-based vegetation. This place is tough for the character, as the mobs (enemies) are extremely powerful here. Clocks go crazy in the Nether, so it is impossible to tell time. It is as if time is slipping away from you.

The third dimension is The End. The goal of survival mode is to reach this final dimension. The End has no day or night cycle and is lit by a glow. Clocks do not keep track of time, just like in the Nether.

The End is where the Ender Dragon, the game's ultimate boss, spawns.

We as Christians should know that there are three dimensions that we can end up in as well.

We start on Earth. Whether we survive and complete the mission in our time on Earth determines what other dimensions we will be visiting. Earth is like the Overworld in Minecraft.

The second dimension we are familiar with is Hell. It is a lake of fire designed to keep Satan and his followers, including us if we fail to rely on God, imprisoned for all eternity. Hell is very similar to the Nether in Minecraft.

8 But the cowardly, the unbelieving,
the vile, the murderers, the
sexually immoral, those who
practice magic arts, the idolaters
and all liars—they will be consigned
to the fiery lake of burning sulfur.
This is the second death.
- Revelation 21:8 (NIV)

The last dimension that we may reach is Heaven. Like The End in Minecraft, time is irrelevant because you will be in eternity. There is no day or night because Jesus will be our constant light, a glow for the city.

The City doesn't need sun or moon
for light. God's Glory is its light, the
Lamb its lamp! The nations will
walk in its light and Earth's kings
bring in their splendor. Its gates will
never be shut by day, and there
won't be any night.
- Revelation 21:23 (MSG)

The Bible talks about a revolt that will take place on the New Earth. The dragon, AKA Satan, leads the revolution and attempts to overthrow God.

7 When the thousand years are over, Satan will be released from his prison and will go out to deceive the nations in the four corners of the Earth... and to gather them for battle...

But fire came down from Heaven and devoured them. 10 And the devil, who deceived them, was thrown into the lake of burning sulfur
- Revelation 20:7-10 (NIV)

Just like there are three dimensions inside the Minecraft Universe: the Overworld, the Nether, and The End, so too did God create us three dimensions: Earth, Hell, and Heaven. Don't forget it.

#24 Nether vs The End

As we've already discovered, Minecraft has three distinct dimensions for players to explore.

The three dimensions are the Overworld, which is like Earth. The Nether, which is like Hell, and The End, is how the Bible describes Heaven.

When I talked with my kids about Minecraft, they played it extensively while I was a passive observer; it fascinated me how driven they were to find The End.

It seemed like kids would just want to keep playing around in endless gameplay in the Overworld or wreak havoc in the fiery Nether, but my kids wanted to reach The End. I asked them if it was hard to get to The End. Their answer,

"Dad, it is so hard to get to The End."

It was extremely hard for my kids, then ten and six-years-old, to beat the Minecraft survival mode. This intrigued me, so I asked if it was easier to reach the Nether.

"Dad, it's so easy to reach the Nether."

The Bible talks about how difficult it is for someone to reach Heaven.

13 "You can enter God's Kingdom only through the narrow gate. The highway to Hell is broad, and its gate is wide for the many who choose that way.

14 But the gateway to life is very narrow and the road is difficult, and only a few ever find it.
- Matthew 7:13-14 (NIV)

Jesus was ultra-clear that getting to Heaven is difficult, but ending up in Hell is pretty straightforward. All you have to do to end up in Hell is keep doing whatever you are doing, but to end up in Heaven, repent, confess that Jesus is Lord, turn around, and change.

9 for, if you confess with your mouth that Jesus is Lord and believe in your heart that God raised him from the dead, you will be saved.
- Romans 10:9 (ESV)

It sounds simple, but it's hard. It takes giving up everything we are and exchanging it for everything God wants us to become.

One man came up and asked Jesus what it would take to get to Heaven, AKA to gain eternal life. Jesus gave him some basic laws and commandments, and the man said,

---

20 "All these I have kept," the young man said. "What do I still lack?"

21 Jesus answered, "If you want to be perfect, go, sell your possessions and give to the poor, and you will have treasure in Heaven. Then come, follow me."

22 When the young man heard this, he went away sad, because he had great wealth.

23 Then Jesus said to his disciples, "Truly I tell you, it is hard for someone who is rich to enter the kingdom of Heaven.

24 Again I tell you, it is easier for a camel to go through the eye of a needle than for someone who is rich to enter the kingdom of God."
Matthew 19:20-24 (NIV)

Just like it is harder to get to The End than it is to reach the Nether in Minecraft, so too is it harder to repent and reach Heaven than to spend eternity in Hell.

#25 Villagers vs Illagers

You are running across the plains sword in hand, the breeze at your back, and sun in your face. The smell of rotting flesh is strong, and you are looking for a place to lay your head as nightfall is approaching.

You see a village off in the distance.
"Yes!" you say as you pick up speed. "A proper house and good trading await."

As you get closer, you see a crowd of people around the entrance to the village. You approach, excited to be in the company of villagers and not mobs for a change.

You walk up and proudly say,

"Hello!"

The crowd stops and looks at you. Something isn't right with these people. They don't look so friendly. And why can't you see anyone inside of the village? You scan the crowd and notice they all have gray eyes. Except for one, he has blue eyes

They turn to you, and you hear a spooky noise,

"Huun!"

You see a bar that is slowly filling up on the screen that says, "Raid."

It turns out these aren't villagers. Instead, they are Illagers (with an "i" for those seeing three L's). Illagers turn out to be one of the mobs or bad guys inside the world of Minecraft.

Villagers are a friendly group of people that live in villages, while Illagers are a band of raiding mobs that want nothing more than to make your life hard. Players consider the villagers "good" and the Illagers "bad."

It isn't always easy to tell from a distance which is which. Villager and Illagers are both characters, and until you see their actions, you may not be too sure which is which.

The Bible talks about two different groups of people and references them as wheat and tares,

---

24 Another parable He put forth to them, saying: "The kingdom of Heaven is like a man who sowed good seed in his field;

25 but while men slept, his enemy came and sowed tares among the wheat and went his way.

26 But when the grain had sprouted and produced a crop, then the tares also appeared.
- Matthew 13:24-26 (NKJV)

Tares are a weed that, at first glance, looks like wheat until it matures. When it's time for harvest, it becomes clear whether the plant is wheat or a tare. While growing, the tares steal the wheat's nutrients and make it more difficult for the wheat to make it to harvest.

Inside our world and our churches, some people may
appear to be growing and maturing in Christ. They appear
to be spiritually healthy, but not every person inside the
church is a healthy crop.

Jesus offers a clue of how to pick out false profits and
tares inside of the church.

The easiest way to tell a tare from wheat is by the crop it is producing. Make sure you are focusing on God and look at what type of fruit you are producing. Is it healthy, godly fruit? Or could your fruit be better? God is always waiting to change you from a tare into wheat. All it takes is for you to repent and ask for His forgiveness.

Just like Illagers and Villagers look similar, but act very different, so too are there tares, people following God in words only, and wheat, those that are following Him in action. Which are you going to choose to be?

#26 Planting

Are you ready to work? Want to be a farmer? Great! There are some fun games that simulate gardening, farming, raising animals, fishing, harvesting, or collecting scarecrows. (if that is your thing)

From the legendary Harvest Moon, the one-man sensation of Stardew Valley, the cute Animal Crossing, to the serious agriculture sim Farming Simulator, video games are not just about beating bad guys. It can be about building a village, growing a crop, or naming your pig.

People can spend hours and even days learning how to carefully plan their farm, plant, water, harvest, and trade their crops. Learning how to care for the things you plant and grow is vital to the crop's health and your farm's success.

Don't place trees too close to each other. Make sure you don't fall on the crops! Add water to speed up growth. Are you growing the best crops for trading? Don't forget to harvest!

Farming tasks revolve around planting the right things in the right places and caring for them until the plants bring a harvest, also known as sowing and reaping.

God tells us to be careful of what we are sowing because we will get more of what we plant.

7 Do not be deceived: God cannot be mocked. A man reaps what he sows.

8 Whoever sows to please their flesh, from the flesh will reap destruction; whoever sows to please the Spirit, from the Spirit will reap eternal life.

*9 Let us not become weary in doing good, for at the proper time we will reap a harvest if we do not give up
- Galatians 6:7-9 (NIV)*

Who wants to harvest a great big pile of destruction? Not me! Then we should be careful not to sow to our flesh. Want to have a lovely barn full of eternal life? Well then, let us choose to sow to the spirit.

*And those who are peacemakers will plant seeds of peace and reap a harvest of righteousness.
- James 3:18 (NLT)*

Anyone who wants to reap righteousness or right living in their lives step right up! We've got some seeds of peace right here.

Just like these games reward you for farming, so too does God reward sowing good seeds with spiritual fruit in our lives.

#27 I'm Waiting

Nintendo and Mario mania enchanted the video gaming world. Mario had a new platform he was saving the world on, the SNES (Super Nintendo Entertainment System), also known as the Super Nintendo. It seemed as if nothing could compete with Nintendo's dominance in the video game industry.

A company named Sega rose to challenge Nintendo. They knew if they wanted to compete with the "Super Nintendo" they'd basically be competing with Mario and need their own hero.

The result was a high-speed game with a little blue ball rolling around. That little blue ball was Sega's star super-speed hero named Sonic. Sonic enabled the Sega Genesis to keep up with Nintendo.

Sonic has been a staple of video game culture ever since and continues to relevant even 30 years later. The speed ball has since called a truce with Mario and appears on multiple games with his former rival, such as Mario & Sonic at the Olympic Games.

Sonic clocks in at a blazing 767mph. Now that is fast. One of his signature lines he uses to taunt the game's bad guy, Eggman, is "I'm waaaiiiting."

The Bible is full of crazy stories, but one of my favorites is when God gave His prophet Elijah super-speed.

Elijah has just been a part of a miracle. He previously had proclaimed a drought was coming and for years there was no rain. He shows back up and challenges the prophets of Baal and wins by calling fire down from heaven.

Now Elijah is praying to God for the rain to return. He's promised the king of the land, Ahab, that God would indeed return the rain.

Elijah climbed to the top of Mount Carmel, bent down to the ground and put his face between his knees and in between praying asks his servant to look for rain.

---

43 "Go and look toward the sea,"
he told his servant. And he went up
and looked.

"There is nothing there," he said.
Seven times Elijah said, "Go back."

44 The seventh time the servant
reported, "A cloud as small as a
man's hand is rising from the sea."
So Elijah said, "Go and tell Ahab,
'Hitch up your chariot and go down
before the rain stops you.'"
1st Kings 18:43-44 (NIV)

Elijah is telling King Ahab to hurry so his chariot doesn't get stuck in the mud when it rains.

God filled Elijah with His spirit and apparently, Elijah got a little excited. You can imagine you've called fire down from heaven and now God is going to bring rain for the first time in years. Watch what happens when God's spirit falls on His servant and he acts,

45 Meanwhile, the sky grew black with clouds, the wind rose, a heavy rain started falling and Ahab rode off to Jezreel.

46 The power of the Lord came on Elijah and, tucking his cloak into his belt, he ran ahead of Ahab all the way to Jezreel.
1st Kings 18:45-46 (NIV)

OK, so big deal, God's prophet Elijah runs and beats king Ahab's chariot. First off, chariots go around 35mph. The fastest human on the planet today, Usain Bolt, ran 27.8mph for 9.5 seconds. He only ran 100 meters and Elijah outran a chariot going 35mph for over 30 miles!

I can just picture the surprise on Ahab's face when Elijah comes walking out of Jezreel and says, "I'm waaaiiiting."

Just like Sega created a hedgehog capable of super-speed to help them with their mission of catching Nintendo, so too does God give us what we need, including super-speed, to help Him in His mission of catching the lost.

#28 Gotta Catch 'Em All

In 1995 a new video game series was created that would take over the video game world and invade our culture on a level that is rarely seen.

The game was Pocket Monsters. It involved human trainers who would catch pocket monsters and train them to fight each other as a sport.

This video game series has now become the 2nd most popular video game series of all time. Having earned $90 billion worldwide, (according to TitleMax.com), it is by far the biggest money earning video game series of all time. To most of us, this game is known as Pokémon.

One thing that made Pokémon stand out in the beginning was the message, Gotta Catch 'Em All. The goal of the game is simple, but difficult. In 1995, your job as a Pokémon trainer was to roam around the Pokemon universe and capture all 151 Pokémon.

You could make it easier by trading Pokémon with your friends. You did this by connecting your Gameboy systems together and swapping Pokémon you'd caught.

This gameplay feature, along with the compelling storyline and brilliance of making you buy two games to complete the mission, propelled Pokémon to its fast rise. Now today twenty-five years later the message is still resonating with new fans of this video game franchise.

The message, complete with theme song, Gotta Catch 'Em All, is a powerful message that Jesus was proclaiming over two thousand years ago.

18 And Jesus came and said to them, "All authority in heaven and on earth has been given to me.

*19 Go therefore and make disciples of **all** nations, baptizing them in the name of the Father and of the Son and of the Holy Spirit,*

20 teaching them to observe all that I have commanded you. And behold, I am with you always, to the end of the age."
- Matthew 28:16-20 (ESV)
(emphasis added)

The mission is intense, it is massive, and we can't do it on our own. Working together as the body of Christ is the only way that we'll be able to reach the entire world with the love of Jesus. We'll need to link up just like players of Pokémon linked up to help each other accomplish the mission.

Jesus never intended for any person to get left behind. He never desired for anyone to go to hell. The Bible makes it clear,

The Lord isn't really being slow about his promise, as some people think. No, he is being patient for your sake. He does not want anyone to be destroyed, but wants

everyone to repent.
- 2 Peter 3:9 (NLT)

There are four lines near the beginning of the Pokémon theme song, Gotta Catch 'Em All, that I think speaks perfectly to the heart that God wants us to have.

To catch them is my real test,
To train them is my cause.
I will travel across the land,
Searching far and wide.

Just like the goal of the video game, Pokémon, is to catch all the pocket monsters, so too is God's goal for each of us is to become catchers of men.

Catching the lost is my real test,
To train them is my eternal cause.

#29 Changing of Costumes

In 2002 there was a game released that bridged the gap between a serious storyline that engaged adults and the fun, lighthearted characters that kids knew and loved.

The creators of the Final Fantasy series, Square Enix, created a game that combined the best of their RPG gaming with some of the most beloved characters of all time. Characters that could compete in popularity with Mario or Sonic. The answer? A mouse. Not just any mouse, but the mouse.

Mickey Mouse and his fun-loving gang crossed over into RPG gaming in the now hit video game series, Kingdom Hearts.

The story is about a 14-year-old boy named Sora who was separated from his friends and his land consumed by darkness. Along with Sora's friends disappearing, Mickey Mouse, the King of Disney Castle, has also gone missing.

Sora must use his newly gained Keyblade, a sword that looks like a key, to fight the bad guys. The bad guys are called Heartless and are a part of the darkness.

As Sora seeks to eliminate the darkness, he must travel to different worlds on his quest. The game bases each of them on famous Disney movies. To fit in, Sora and his counterparts, Donald and Goofy, must change their appearance to match the world they find themselves in.

Atlantica is based on the Little Mermaid. There Sora must dress as a Merman. In the Pirates of the Caribbean World Sora dresses like a pirate. When he visits the Pride Lands from the Lion King, he changes into a lion. When he visits Monsters Inc., he becomes a, well, you probably get the idea.

Sora becomes what he needs to be to accomplish the mission in the geographic region he finds himself. Sora must give up who he normally is to become who he needs to be in order to save his friends that are lost.

God calls us to do the same. In 1st Corinthians Paul explains how he uses his freedom to save those he encounters,

19 Though I am free and belong to no one, I have made myself a slave to everyone, to win as many as possible.

20 To the Jews I became like a Jew, to win the Jews. To those under the law I became like one under the law (though I myself am not under the law), so as to win those under the law.

21 To those not having the law I became like one not having the law (though I am not free from God's law but am under Christ's law), so as to win those not having the law.

22 To the weak I became weak, to win the weak. **I have become all things to all people so that by all possible means I might save some.**

23 I do all this for the sake of the gospel, that I may share in its

Paul would change his approach to reach the lost. Paul was a Jew and knew their culture well, but when he lived and talked with non-Jews, known as Gentiles, Paul matched and lived within their customs and culture.

Sometimes when we are trying to reach the lost, we must forget who we are so that we might save some.

This seems counter-intuitive, especially in our culture. We celebrate you being "you," being true to yourself, believing in yourself, and we are encouraged to find ourselves.

God though has a different viewpoint.

Then Jesus said to his disciples, "If any of you wants to be my follower, you must give up your own way, take up your cross, and follow me. 25 If you try to hang on to your life, you will lose it. But if you give up your life for my sake, you will save it.
- Matthew 16:24-25 (NLT)

If there is someone God has brought into your life that you need to reach, forget who you are and become who Jesus is calling you to be to reach that person. You may love to eat a good juicy burger, but when you visit a friend who is vegan, you may need to grab a handful of nuts and tell them about Jesus.

Just like the creators of Kingdom Hearts made Sora change his costumes to match the world he found himself in, so too did God give us the ability and permission to lose ourselves in order to reach our friends and others that are lost.

#30 Legendary Like Zelda

An evil demon has captured the princess and stole her away. With a mighty sword, the hero races after her.

In 1986, Shigeru Miyamoto, the lead creator of Super Mario Bros. helped create the Legend of Zelda.

The story was about a young man that is called to save the kingdom of Hyrule from the evil demon Ganon. The hero is reincarnated throughout time, whenever he is needed. His name is Link.

Link has become one of the most famous video game characters and players love him for his pointy ears, sword, and who can forget his flower bombs.

The people of Hyrule have prophecies about Link. They pass down the tale of the Hero of Time from generation to generation.

> "I had a dream… In the dream, dark storm clouds were billowing over the land of Hyrule… But suddenly, a ray of light shot out of the forest, parted the clouds and lit up the ground… The light turned into a figure holding a green and shining stone, followed by a fairy. I know this is a prophecy that someone would come from the forest…" – Princess Zelda

The Old Testament in the Bible, which is filled with ancient writings prior to Jesus arrival, has over four hundred prophesies foreshadowing the birth, death, burial, and resurrection of Jesus Christ. These were prophecies about what they called the coming Messiah, the savior of the

Jews. They thought the Messiah was going to come and deliver them from Rome and other oppressors.

"Here is my servant, whom I uphold, my chosen one in whom I delight; I will put my Spirit on him, and he will bring justice to the nations.

2 He will not shout or cry out, or raise his voice in the streets.

3 A bruised reed he will not break, and a smoldering wick he will not snuff out. In faithfulness he will bring forth justice;

4 he will not falter or be discouraged till he establishes justice on earth.
- Isaiah 42:1-4 (NIV)

For the Jews who felt they were being treated unjustly, this savior was exactly what they needed. Someone to make the world just again.

We now know that Jesus came not as a warrior, but as a spiritual savior, but for all of us who experience pain, suffering, and unjust circumstances, the Legend of Jesus is something we can hold on to.

In Revelation, a book filled with prophecies about how Jesus will return, He promises to come back in splendid fashion.

11 Now I saw heaven opened, and behold, a white horse. And He who sat on him was called Faithful and True, and in righteousness He judges and makes war.

12 His eyes were like a flame of fire, and on His head were many crowns. He had a name written that no one knew except Himself.

13 He was clothed with a robe dipped in blood, and His name is called The Word of God.

14 And the armies in heaven, clothed in fine linen, white and clean, followed Him on white horses.

15 Now out of His mouth goes a sharp sword, that with it He should strike the nations. And He Himself will rule them with a rod of iron. He Himself treads the winepress of the fierceness and wrath of Almighty God.

16 And He has on His robe and on His thigh a name written:

*KING OF KINGS AND
LORD OF LORDS.
- Revelation 19:11-16 (NIV)*

Jesus is coming back and for all of us who are eager for His return, He promises us,

---

12 "Look, I am coming soon! My reward is with me, and I will give to each person according to what they have done.

*13 I am the Alpha and the Omega, the First and the Last, the Beginning and the End.
- Revelation 22:12-13 (NIV)*

Just like Link was prophesied as the Hero of Time, so too was Jesus, the true time traveling hero that has been prophesied about for millenniums. He is coming back to save His people and to rule His kingdom. He is the Alpha and the Omega, the Beginning and the End, God is Legendary.

Final Thoughts

The landscape of entertainment has changed over the past four decades through video games. Now people more than ever want to participate in the story rather than just watch it on a screen. Video games satisfy the desire for someone who wants to be a part of story, who wants to be a hero, for someone that wants to make a difference.

We have a God given drive to save the damsel in distress like Mario or Link, to save our friends like Sora, or to save the world like Cloud. That we can ever say, "I want to change the world" as kids and adults is audacious, but I believe God has put into us a God sized ambition for His kingdom, His story, and to help save His creation.

The world needs saving. Every day Satan and his evil minions are capturing people and lying to them. They are being told they aren't worth anything. That no one loves them and that life isn't worth living. They are being told that God isn't real, that we are gods ourselves and it is all a lie.

God has given us the ultimate mission, to reach the entire world with His love. Nothing can save the world or is more heroic than sharing the gospel of Christ. God has called us to love those around us.

12 My command is this: Love each other as I have loved you. 13 Greater love has no one than this: to lay down one's life for one's friends. 14 You are my friends if you do what I command.
- John 15:12-13 (NIV)

The world is a dark place and people that love stand out. When people are used to being lied to by the world, a person who speaks the truth in love, becomes someone people want to be around. It is hard to figure out how to navigate through this world, and we as Christians provide light and direction for those who are lost.

14 "You are the light of the world. A town built on a hill cannot be hidden.

15 Neither do people light a lamp and put it under a bowl. Instead they put it on its stand, and it gives light to everyone In the house.

16 In the same way, let your light shine before others, that they may see your good deeds and glorify your Father In heaven.
- Matthew 5:14-16 (NIV)

God is weaving an amazing story together that He wants you to be a part of. He has all his characters in place. He sent Jesus the savior of the world to fight the evil fallen angel Lucifer, to rescue the world from its coming destruction.

He has equipped us with weapons, armor, special abilities, and a strategy guide. The mission is on a scale that the

World of Warcraft can only gawk at. The world is open for us to explore, filled with Easter Eggs and side quests that God has orchestrated. There are interesting characters all along the way that'll help, entertain, and frustrate you in your journey.

The bad guys are real, the need is great, and only you, the chosen ones, can go save the world from the darkness that is closing in.

---

9 But you are a chosen generation, a royal priesthood, a holy nation, His own special people, that you may proclaim the praises of Him who called you out of darkness into His marvelous light;
- 1 Peter 2:9 (NKJV)

All you need to embark on this amazing journey is to "Press Start" by stepping foot outside your door. God is calling you, God has equipped you, God has empowered you, God is Like a Video Game.

Made in the USA
Middletown, DE
28 May 2023

31628579R00060